Notes

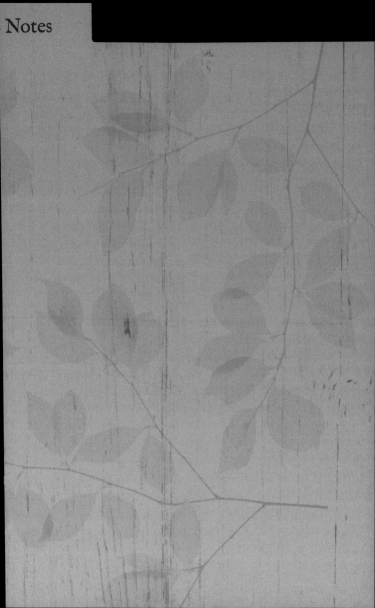

Notes

Notes

Notes

To Do

- Math Lesson 38 ☐
- Spelling ☐
- Clean Room ☐
- Get mom/dad to see if I can go to danereá's laser tag b-day party ☐

To Do

To Do

To Do

To Do

To Do

To Do

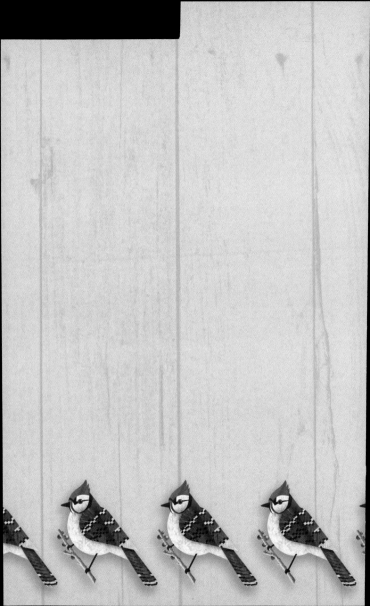

To Do

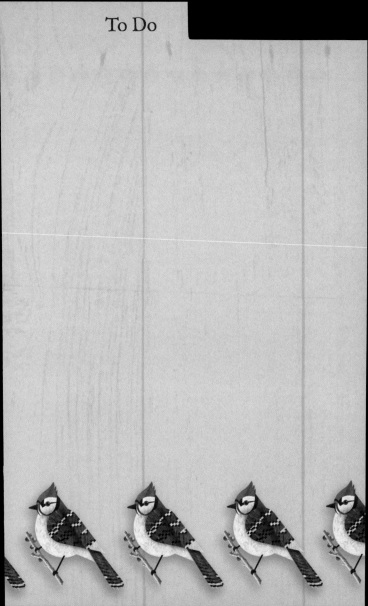

To Do

To Do

To Do

Ideas

- Operation Christmas Child: a 'have hope' neclace of some sort.

- Toothbrush, toothpaste, w/ candy attached

- Cash donation

Ideas

Ideas

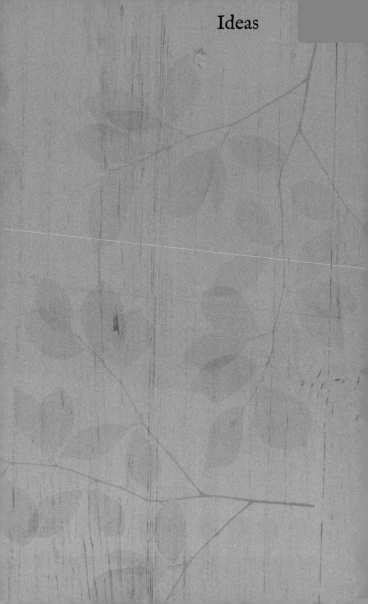

Ideas

Ideas

Ideas

Ideas

Ideas

Ideas

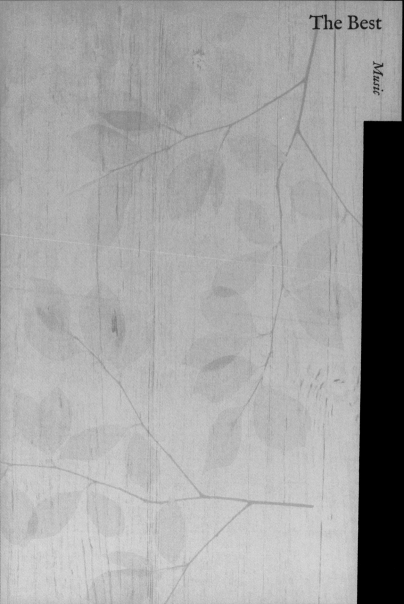

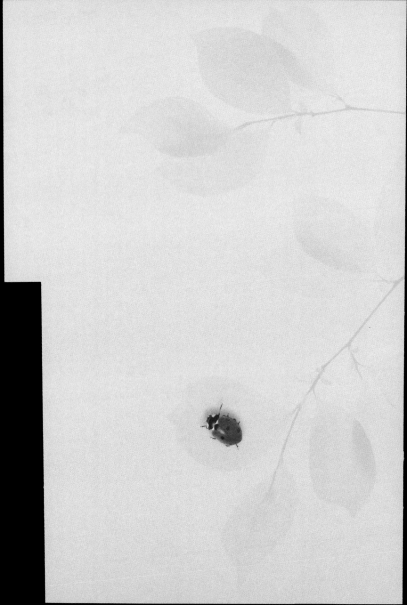

The Best

Websites

The Best

Restaurants

Emma

a-Laa-La-La-La-Laa-La-La-La-La-La-La
La-La-La-La-La. The outro for "Chris
Wish rang in my ear. I shove of m
covers and hop out of bed. "Wake
I tell my twin sister. "Why 5:45 am
she grunts from under her covers.
I grab the clothes I set out yeste
and head downstairs. Nobody else i
up, so I blend a strawberry smoothie,
some toast, and turn on the T.V.

Emily

Arragh. My sisters alarm goes off at
5:45 and she is already downstair
After she eats she will come up here